QUICKBOOKS ONLINE FOR SENIORS

A Simple, Step-by-Step Guide to Managing Finances and Tracking Expenses—Easy-to-Follow, Large Print, and Jargon-Free! Designed for seniors andNon-Tech-Savvy Users!

Finn Wilder

INTRODUCTION

If you've picked up this guide, chances are you're ready to take control of your personal or small business finances—but you want to do it in a way that's simple, easy to understand, and not filled with confusing tech talk. First of all, *congratulations*! You're about to learn a powerful tool that can help you stay organized, save time, and reduce stress when it comes to managing money.

This book was written *just for you*—the senior who might not feel "tech-savvy" or the retiree who wants to learn how to keep track of income and expenses without the hassle. Whether you're managing rental income, running a small business, helping with family finances, or simply wanting to keep your personal spending in order, you're in the right place.

Why This Book is Different: Large Print, Plain Language, and Simple Steps

We know that most financial and accounting books are written with small print, complex jargon, and assume you already know how to use modern apps and tools. That's not helpful—and it's not what you'll find here.

This guide uses:

- **Large, easy-to-read print**

- **Clear, step-by-step instructions**

- **Screenshots and visual cues**

- **No complicated tech terms—just real talk**

Every explanation is made with *you* in mind. No overwhelming lingo, no assumptions. Just a helpful, friendly voice walking you through everything in simple, plain English. And when a financial term *does* come up, don't worry—there's a bonus glossary included just for that!

What is QuickBooks Online and Why It's Useful?

QuickBooks Online is a web-based accounting program designed to help you track money coming in and going out, keep your finances organized, and make tax season easier. The best part? You don't have to install anything complicated. You can access QuickBooks from your computer, tablet, or even your phone—anytime, anywhere.

With QuickBooks, you can:

- Create and send invoices

- Record and categorize expenses

- Track payments and income

- Run easy-to-read financial reports

- Connect your bank account for automatic updates

And you don't need to be an accountant or a tech genius to use it. This guide will help you understand everything you need to know—at *your* pace.

Overview of What You'll Learn

This book breaks down QuickBooks Online into easy-to-follow parts. You'll learn:

- **How to set up your account** in minutes

- **How to navigate the dashboard** with confidence

- **How to record income and track expenses** without feeling lost

- **How to generate useful reports** to keep tabs on your finances

- **How to collaborate with family or a bookkeeper** if needed

- **How to troubleshoot problems** and keep your information safe

And for your convenience, you'll also get **3 helpful bonuses**:

1. A **Quick Start Checklist** to keep by your desk

2. A **Jargon-Free Glossary** of common terms

3. A **Large-Print Keyboard Shortcuts Cheat Sheet** to save you time

This is your go-to companion for mastering QuickBooks Online the simple, stress-free way.

How to Use This Guide (Tips for Beginners)

This guide is designed to be *read at your own pace*. Feel free to start at the beginning and work through each chapter, or skip to the section you need most. Each chapter is written to stand on its own, so you're never stuck if you decide to jump around.

Here are a few helpful tips to get the most out of this book:

- **Keep it handy while using QuickBooks Online**—use it as your on-screen helper.

- **Highlight or write notes** in the margins as you go.

- **Use the Bonus Glossary** whenever a word feels unfamiliar.

- **Take your time**—you're not in a race. Learning something new should be empowering, not overwhelming.

You've got this—and we're going to walk through it together, one clear, friendly step at a time.

So, take a deep breath, grab a cup of tea or coffee, and let's begin your journey into managing your finances the smart, easy way—with QuickBooks Online.

CHAPTER ONE

Getting Started with QuickBooks Online

Welcome to the first chapter of your journey toward financial empowerment! In this chapter, we'll introduce you to QuickBooks Online, help you choose the best plan to suit your needs, and walk you through the process of setting up your account—all explained in a friendly, step-by-step manner that's easy to follow.

What is QuickBooks Online?

Imagine having a personal assistant for your finances—someone who helps you keep track of every dollar in and out, organizes your bills, and prepares simple financial reports for you. That's exactly what **QuickBooks Online** does. It's a cloud-based accounting tool designed to simplify money management, whether you're handling personal expenses, small business finances, or rental income.

Key Benefits:

- **Accessibility:** Since it's online, you can access your financial data from your computer, tablet, or smartphone, wherever you are.

- **Organization:** It automatically organizes your income and expenses, so you always know where your money is going.

- **Ease of Use:** With a user-friendly interface, it takes the stress out of accounting by guiding you through each process with simple, clear steps.

- **Security:** Your financial information is securely stored in the cloud, and QuickBooks provides robust protection to keep your data safe.

Think of QuickBooks Online as your digital ledger that not only saves you time but also helps you understand your finances better without overwhelming you with complicated accounting language.

Choosing the Right Plan for Your Needs

QuickBooks Online offers several plans, and finding the right one can feel like choosing a new TV—there are lots of options, but only one (or two) will fit just right. Here's how you can decide:

1. **Assess Your Needs:**
   - **Personal or Small Business:** Are you managing your own finances, or do you have a small

business? The plan you need may differ based on the volume of transactions.

- o **Features You Need:** Consider what features are most important for you. Do you need help with invoicing, tracking expenses, or running reports? Write these down as a checklist.

2. **Plan Options:**

- o **Simple Start:** Ideal for beginners or those with basic needs. It covers invoicing, expense tracking, and basic reporting.

- o **Essentials:** A step up if you need to handle more transactions or require additional features like bill management and time tracking.

- o **Plus:** Best for those with more complex needs, such as managing inventory or generating more detailed financial reports.

3. **Budget Considerations:**

- o Compare the costs of each plan and balance them against the features you actually need. Remember, the goal is to simplify your financial management, not to pay for extra bells and whistles that won't be used.

4. **Free Trials:**

   o QuickBooks Online often offers a free trial period. Use this time to explore the interface and features. This hands-on experience can be very reassuring and help you decide which plan is best suited to your comfort level and needs.

By taking a moment to think about these factors, you'll be in a much better position to choose the plan that fits your lifestyle and financial goals.

Creating and Setting Up Your Account

Now that you have an idea of which plan might work best for you, it's time to set up your account. Follow these simple steps, and remember—there's no rush. Take your time, and feel free to pause and review each step as needed.

Step-by-Step Account Setup

1. **Visit the QuickBooks Online Website:**

   o Open your web browser and type in the QuickBooks Online URL. You'll be greeted by a welcoming home page with options to sign up or start a free trial.

2. **Sign Up for an Account:**

   o Click on the "Sign Up" or "Start Free Trial" button. You'll be prompted to enter basic information such as your name, email address, and a password. Use a password that you can easily remember but is also secure.

3. **Select Your Plan:**

   o After creating your basic profile, you will be asked to choose the plan that best suits your needs. Refer back to your checklist from earlier to help you decide.

4. **Answer a Few Simple Questions:**

   o QuickBooks may ask you a few questions about your business or personal finances. These questions help tailor the experience to your needs. Answer honestly and simply—you're not being tested here!

5. **Set Up Your Profile:**

- Enter your business or personal details, including your address and contact information. This information is important for creating accurate financial records.

- You may be prompted to add a profile picture or company logo if you're setting up a business account. If this feels unnecessary, you can skip it.

6. **Customize Your Dashboard:**

- Once your account is created, take a few minutes to familiarize yourself with the dashboard. You can usually find a "Getting Started" guide within the interface that points out where to find key features like invoicing, expense tracking, and reports.

- Adjust the settings for larger text or a simpler layout if available—this will make your ongoing experience much more comfortable.

7. **Explore the Tutorials and Help Resources:**

- QuickBooks offers built-in tutorials and a help center. Don't hesitate to click on the help button if you need a little extra guidance while setting up your account. These resources are designed to walk you through any challenges step-by-step.

A Guided Tour of the Dashboard

Imagine your QuickBooks Online dashboard as your very own cockpit—simple, clear, and designed just for you. When you first log in, you'll see a screen that may seem busy at a glance, but every section has its purpose. Let's walk through it together.

1. The Home Screen

When you first enter QuickBooks Online, the Home Screen welcomes you. Here's what you typically see:

- **Snapshots of Your Financial Health:** At the top, you might notice a few summary boxes showing your income, expenses, and overall profit. These give you a quick glance at how your finances are doing.

- **Navigation Panel:** Usually located on the left side, this panel is your main menu. It includes links to different areas like Dashboard, Invoices, Expenses, Reports, and more.

- **Activity Feed:** In the center or on one side, there's an activity feed that shows recent transactions or notifications. Think of it as a diary of your recent financial actions.

2. Key Areas You'll Use Frequently

- **Invoices & Sales:** This section lets you create and send invoices, track payments, and review sales. It's designed to be straightforward, with clear buttons and large print options for easy reading.

- **Expenses:** Here, you'll record what you spend. You can upload receipts or enter details manually. The system helps by grouping expenses into categories, so you can see where your money goes.

- **Reports:** This part is like your financial report card. You can generate simple, easy-to-read reports that show your profit and loss, balance sheets, and more. The numbers and charts are presented in a clear, no-nonsense format.

- **Banking:** This section helps you connect your bank account securely, so your transactions can be imported automatically. It's like having a digital bank statement that updates itself.

3. Customizing Your Experience

One of the best parts about QuickBooks Online is that it lets you tailor the dashboard to fit your preferences. If you prefer larger text or a simpler layout:

- **Look for Settings or Preferences:** Often found at the top right or in the navigation panel, these options let you adjust the display settings.

- **Rearrange Widgets:** Many sections of the dashboard are "widgets" that you can move around. Place your most-used features in spots that feel natural to you.

Remember, there's no rush to explore everything all at once. Take your time, click around, and use the "Help" button whenever you need a little extra guidance. Over time, the dashboard will become a familiar and powerful tool in managing your finances.

Understanding the Basic Terminology (Jargon-Free!)

One common obstacle when starting with any new tool is the language. QuickBooks Online uses terms that might sound a bit like a foreign language at first, but don't worry—we're here to explain them in everyday words.

1. Dashboard

- **What It Means:** This is the main screen where you see a snapshot of your financial information.

- **Plain English:** Think of it like the front page of your newspaper—packed with the headlines of what's happening with your money.

2. Transactions

- **What It Means:** Any financial activity, such as payments received, expenses paid, or money moved between accounts.

- **Plain English:** These are the entries in your financial diary. Each time money comes in or goes out, it's recorded as a transaction.

3. Invoices

- **What It Means:** Bills you send to customers to request payment for services or products provided.

- **Plain English:** An invoice is simply a detailed bill that lets someone know how much they owe you.

4. Expenses

- **What It Means:** Money you spend to run your business or manage your personal finances.

- **Plain English:** These are the costs you pay, like bills, supplies, or any other purchases.

5. Reports

- **What It Means:** Summaries and charts that display your financial data.

- **Plain English:** Think of reports as progress reports for your money. They show you the big picture of your income, spending, and overall financial health.

6. Banking

- **What It Means:** The process of linking your bank accounts to QuickBooks Online to import transactions.

- **Plain English:** This is how your bank information gets into QuickBooks automatically, much like syncing your phone with a computer.

7. Categories

- **What It Means:** Labels or groups that you assign to transactions to organize them.

- **Plain English:** Categories are like folders in a filing cabinet, helping you sort your transactions into understandable groups (like groceries, utilities, or rent).

By breaking down these terms into everyday language, we hope you feel more confident and less intimidated. Financial tools don't have to be filled with confusing words—each term is simply a tool to help you understand and control your money better.

CHAPTER TWO

Navigating the Dashboard with Confidence

Welcome back! Now that you've familiarized yourself with the basics of QuickBooks Online and explored the dashboard, it's time to get comfortable with the place where you'll be spending most of your time. In this chapter, we're going to walk through the main features of your dashboard and show you how to customize the layout to suit your personal needs—making everything as simple and clear as possible.

Main Features and What They Do

When you open QuickBooks Online, the dashboard might seem a bit busy at first glance, but every part of it is designed to help you manage your finances with ease. Let's break down the key features and explain what they do in everyday language.

1. Financial Snapshot

- **What It Is:** A quick summary of your income, expenses, and profit.

- **In Plain English:** Think of this as your daily weather report for your money. It shows you at a glance whether your finances are sunny or a bit cloudy.

2. Invoices and Sales Section

- **What It Is:** A dedicated area for creating, sending, and tracking invoices.

- **In Plain English:** This is like your billing counter. It helps you know who owes you money and keeps a record of every bill you've sent out.

3. Expenses Section

- **What It Is:** The place where you enter and track all the money you spend.

- **In Plain English:** Imagine a well-organized filing cabinet where every receipt, bill, or purchase is carefully filed so you can see where your money is going.

4. Reports Section

- **What It Is:** A tool that generates summaries and visual charts of your financial data.

- **In Plain English:** Reports are like your financial progress reports. They give you a big-picture view of how your income and expenses balance out over time.

5. Banking Section

- **What It Is:** The feature that connects your bank account to QuickBooks Online.

- **In Plain English:** This section works like a digital bridge between your bank and your financial records, automatically bringing in your transactions so you don't have to manually input every detail.

6. Activity Feed

- **What It Is:** A log of recent actions and transactions.

- **In Plain English:** Think of this as a timeline or diary that shows all the important financial events as they happen, so you can quickly check what's been updated.

Each of these features is designed to help you stay on top of your financial health. By regularly checking these sections, you'll have a clearer understanding of your money management without feeling overwhelmed.

Customizing the Layout for Simplicity

One of the wonderful aspects of QuickBooks Online is its flexibility. It allows you to tailor the dashboard so that it works best for you. Whether you need larger text or a simplified layout, here's how you can make the dashboard feel like it was built just for you.

1. Adjusting the Display Settings

- **Increase Text Size:** QuickBooks Online offers settings to enlarge text for better readability. Look for the "Settings" or "Preferences" menu—often represented by a gear icon. Here, you might find options to change the font size or select a "large print" mode.

- **Simplify Colors and Contrast:** If you find the default color scheme too busy, adjust the contrast or choose a layout with softer colors. This can reduce visual strain and make the important information stand out.

2. Rearranging Widgets

- **Drag and Drop:** Many sections on your dashboard, like the financial snapshot or activity feed, are presented as widgets that you can easily rearrange. Simply click and hold the title of a widget, then drag it to a position that makes sense for you. *Imagine arranging your favorite photos on a wall—place your most-used features right where you can see them clearly.*

- **Hide Unused Sections:** If there's a feature you're not using, you can often minimize or hide it to declutter your screen. This way, only the most relevant information remains in your view, reducing any potential confusion.

3. Using the Help and Tutorial Options

- **Built-In Guidance:** QuickBooks Online is designed to help you learn as you go. If you're unsure about a setting or a feature, click on the "Help" button—usually found in the upper right corner. You'll find step-by-step tutorials and FAQs tailored to seniors and beginners.

- **Bookmark Your Favorite Settings:** Once you've customized your dashboard, take a moment to bookmark your settings page or jot down the steps. This makes it easy to reapply your favorite layout if you ever need to reset things.

4. Personal Touches for a Comfortable Experience

- **Color Coding:** Some users find that adding a personal touch, like color coding different sections (for example, blue for income and red for expenses), can make a big difference in quickly locating the right information.

- **Layout Consistency:** Try to maintain consistency in the layout across different devices. This way, whether you're on a computer, tablet, or phone, you'll always know where to find your financial summaries.

Customizing your dashboard isn't just about making things look nice—it's about creating an environment that makes you feel confident and in control of your finances. Remember, there's no "one size fits all" here; it's all about what works best for you.

Using the Help Button When You're Stuck

We all encounter moments when something doesn't quite make sense or a new feature seems confusing. The great thing about QuickBooks Online is that you're never truly alone in these moments—help is always just a click away.

Instant Assistance at Your Fingertips

- **Look for the "Help" Icon:** Typically, the Help button is located at the top right corner of your screen. It might look like a small question mark or be labeled "Help." This is your shortcut to a wealth of information.

- **Step-by-Step Tutorials:** When you click on the Help button, you'll find a variety of tutorials and FAQs that explain features in simple, everyday language. These step-by-step guides are tailored to assist beginners and are designed with clarity in mind. Whether you're confused about a particular term or need to understand a process, these resources break everything down into manageable pieces.

- **Search Functionality:** You can type in a question or keywords related to what you're trying to do. For example, if you're having trouble finding the "Expenses" section, simply type "find expenses" into the help search bar. The results will point you to the right resource or article.

- **Live Support and Community Forums:** In addition to the built-in resources, QuickBooks Online often offers live chat support and community forums. These features allow you to connect with both QuickBooks experts and other users who might have faced similar challenges. It's like having a friendly neighbor ready to lend a hand whenever you need it.

Using the Help button is like having a digital assistant by your side. Don't hesitate to click it when you're unsure—the more you use it, the more comfortable you'll become with the platform.

Tips for Seniors: Making Text Larger and Easier to Read

Clear, readable text is crucial for a stress-free experience, especially when managing important financial details. QuickBooks Online offers several features and settings that make it easier for seniors and non-tech-savvy users to view the information comfortably.

Adjusting the Text Size

- **Built-In Display Settings:** Within QuickBooks Online, look for a settings menu—often represented by a gear icon. In this menu, you'll find options to adjust the font size or switch to a "large print" mode. Increasing the text size can significantly improve readability, reducing eye strain and making navigation a breeze.

- **Browser Zoom:** If you can't find an option within QuickBooks itself, don't worry. Your web browser also offers a simple way to enlarge the text. Simply press Ctrl and + on a Windows computer or Command and + on a Mac. This zooms in on the entire webpage, making all text and icons larger. Most browsers also let you set a default zoom level so that every time you log in, the page appears in your preferred size.

Customizing the Layout for Easier Reading

- **Simplified Display Options:** Beyond just increasing text size, consider choosing a layout that minimizes clutter. QuickBooks Online often allows you to rearrange or hide certain elements on your dashboard. By prioritizing the information you use most and removing unnecessary visual noise, you create a clearer, more focused workspace.

- **High Contrast Mode:** If you find it challenging to read text against the background, look for a high contrast option in your display settings. High contrast mode can help make the text pop, which is especially useful for users with vision difficulties.

- **Bookmarking and Shortcuts:** For features you use frequently, consider bookmarking them in your browser or setting up desktop shortcuts. This reduces the need for repetitive navigation through menus and makes your overall experience smoother.

Practical Reminders for a Comfortable Experience

- **Take Your Time:** Remember that it's perfectly okay to take things slowly. Spend a few minutes adjusting these settings until you're comfortable. The goal is to create an environment that feels right for you.

- **Experiment with Settings:** Every individual's needs are unique. Don't be afraid to experiment with different display and layout options until you find the perfect combination. Your comfort is the key to mastering QuickBooks Online.

Wrapping Up

By now, you've learned how to use the Help button as a trusty guide when questions arise and discovered practical tips to make the text larger and easier to read. These adjustments are designed to enhance your comfort and ensure that every time you interact with QuickBooks Online, you feel supported and in control.

Take a moment to explore these features at your own pace. The more you customize your experience, the more natural it will feel. Remember, every click and setting change is a step towards a smoother, more confident journey in managing your finances.

Keep moving forward with the confidence that you're building a financial tool that's truly designed for you—simple, clear, and empowering.

CHAPTER THREE

Managing Income the Easy Way

Welcome to Chapter 3! In this section, we're going to simplify the process of handling your income. Whether you're a small business owner, a freelancer, or just managing your personal income, this chapter is designed to make creating invoices, tracking payments, recording sales, and understanding your financial reports as easy and stress-free as possible. Let's break down each step in clear, simple language.

Creating and Sending Invoices

Imagine an invoice as a friendly reminder—a clear, written note that tells someone how much they owe you for goods or services. QuickBooks Online makes this process straightforward, even if you're new to digital invoicing.

- **Easy-to-Use Templates:** QuickBooks Online offers pre-designed invoice templates that you can personalize with your name, logo (if you have one), and contact details. You don't need any design skills—the templates are already laid out in a clear, large-print format that's perfect for easy reading.

- **Step-by-Step Creation:** Simply click on the "Create Invoice" button, and follow the on-screen prompts. You'll fill in details like:

  - The customer's name and contact information.

  - A description of the product or service.

  - The amount owed.

  - The due date for payment.

- **Sending Made Simple:** Once your invoice is ready, you can send it directly through QuickBooks Online via email. If you prefer, you can also print a copy to mail or hand-deliver it. This flexibility ensures you can choose the method that feels most comfortable for you.

Tip: Save a copy of your template so you can reuse it for future invoices, saving you time and making the process even simpler.

Tracking Customer Payments

After sending out your invoices, the next step is tracking the payments as they come in. QuickBooks Online keeps this process clear and organized.

- **Automatic Updates:** When a customer makes a payment, QuickBooks Online updates the invoice status automatically. This means you can easily see which invoices are paid, pending, or overdue without having to manually check each one.

- **Payment Reminders:** The system can send automatic reminders to customers who haven't paid by the due date. This gentle nudge helps ensure you receive your money on time, without the need for you to make uncomfortable follow-up calls.

- **Clear Visual Indicators:** Look for visual cues on your dashboard, like color-coded statuses (for example, green for paid, yellow for pending, and red for overdue). These icons make it easy to understand the state of your payments at a glance.

Tip: Regularly check your payment tracking section to stay on top of your cash flow. It's like a quick daily checkup for your finances.

Recording Sales and Income Without Stress

Recording your sales and income should be a simple task, not a source of stress. QuickBooks Online is designed to capture your transactions accurately and with minimal effort.

- **Automatic Data Capture:** If you have your bank account linked, QuickBooks Online can import your transactions automatically. This means you won't have to manually enter every single sale—saving you time and reducing the chance for errors.

- **Manual Entries:** For those times when you need to enter sales manually (maybe for cash transactions or sales made outside of your usual channels), the process is straightforward. Just click on "Add Sale" or "Record Income," fill in the details, and save. The system is built to handle each entry with clear, large-print fields that are easy to read and understand.

- **Categorizing for Clarity:** As you record income, you can assign categories or tags to each sale (like "product sales," "service fees," or "rental income"). This helps keep your finances organized and makes it easier to review later.

Tip: Take a few minutes at the end of each week to review your sales entries. Regular updates help prevent mistakes and keep your financial records accurate.

Viewing Reports That Make Sense

Reports are your financial progress reports—they help you see how well you're doing and where your money is coming from. QuickBooks Online turns your raw data into easy-to-read reports that speak in plain language.

- **Simple Financial Snapshots:** Reports like Profit & Loss and Income Statements are designed to show you, in clear terms, the overall health of your finances. You'll see total income, expenses, and the net profit (or loss) in a layout that's easy to follow.

- **Visual Aids:** Many reports include charts or graphs that visually represent your data. These can help you quickly understand trends, such as increases in income or unexpected dips in sales, without needing to decipher complex tables of numbers.

- **Customizable Time Frames:** You can view your reports over different periods—daily, weekly, monthly, or yearly. This flexibility allows you to monitor your financial progress over time and spot patterns that might help you plan for the future.

- **Large Print and Clear Labels:** The reports are designed with clarity in mind. With larger text and straightforward labeling, you'll be able to read your financial data without any hassle.

Tip: Start by reviewing your reports at the end of each month. This habit not only keeps you informed but also gives you the confidence to make small adjustments that can lead to big improvements in your financial management.

Wrapping Up

Managing your income doesn't have to be complicated. With QuickBooks Online, creating and sending invoices, tracking payments, recording sales, and viewing easy-to-understand reports are all designed to fit into your daily routine without adding extra stress. By taking these steps one at a time, you'll build a solid foundation for managing your finances confidently.

Remember, this guide is here to support you every step of the way. Take your time, explore each feature, and soon managing your income will become as natural as reading your favorite newspaper. Keep going—you're doing a great job taking control of your financial future!

CHAPTER FOUR

Tracking Expenses Without Headaches

Welcome to Chapter 4, where we take a deep breath and simplify the process of keeping track of your spending. Managing expenses might seem like a daunting task, but with QuickBooks Online, it becomes a friendly, straightforward part of your day. In this chapter, we'll walk you through how to securely connect your bank account to automatically import your transactions and, when needed, how to manually enter your expenses in a clear, stress-free way.

Connecting Your Bank Account Safely

One of the biggest advantages of QuickBooks Online is its ability to link directly to your bank account. This connection takes the hassle out of entering every single transaction by automatically importing your expenses. Here's how you can do it safely and confidently:

Why Connect Your Bank Account?

- **Automatic Updates:** Linking your bank account means that every time you make a purchase, it can be automatically recorded in your QuickBooks Online account. This saves you the time of manually logging each expense and reduces the chance of errors.

- **Real-Time Tracking:** With your bank transactions flowing into your system, you get an up-to-date picture of your spending. This helps you keep better track of your finances and spot any discrepancies quickly.

Steps to Connect Your Bank Account

1. **Find the Banking Section:** Once you're logged in, navigate to the "Banking" tab on the left-hand side of your dashboard. This is where you'll set up your bank connection.

2. **Select Your Bank:** QuickBooks Online will present you with a list of popular banks. If you see your bank on the list, simply select it. If not, you can use the search function to find it.

3. **Enter Your Credentials Securely:** You'll be prompted to enter your online banking username and password. Rest assured, QuickBooks uses advanced encryption technology to keep your information safe. If you have any doubts, check with your bank to understand their security measures.

4. **Review and Confirm:** Once connected, review the transactions that are imported to ensure everything looks correct. QuickBooks Online does its best to match the transactions with your existing records, but it's always good to give it a quick once-over.

Safety Tips for Peace of Mind

- **Use Strong Passwords:** Make sure both your bank and QuickBooks accounts are protected by strong, unique passwords.

- **Enable Two-Factor Authentication:** If available, add an extra layer of security to your accounts by enabling two-factor authentication. This means that even if someone gets hold of your password, they'll need a second form of verification to access your account.

- **Monitor Regularly:** Regularly check your account for any unfamiliar transactions. QuickBooks makes it easy to spot changes, and you can address them immediately if something doesn't look right.

Connecting your bank account is a fantastic way to take the stress out of expense tracking. With automatic updates and robust security measures in place, you can focus more on understanding your finances and less on manual data entry.

Manually Entering Expenses

While automatic bank feeds are incredibly useful, there may be times when you need to enter an expense manually—perhaps for cash purchases, receipts that aren't linked to your account, or occasional expenses made on the go. QuickBooks Online makes this process as straightforward as possible.

When to Enter Expenses Manually

- **Cash Transactions:** Not every expense will come directly from your bank account. For cash purchases or expenses paid in person, manual entry ensures your records stay complete.

- **Receipts and Invoices:** If you receive a paper receipt or invoice that isn't automatically imported, you can easily add it to QuickBooks Online.

Steps for Manual Entry

1. **Navigate to the Expenses Section:** From your dashboard, click on "Expenses" or "Transactions." This is your central hub for recording any spending that isn't automatically imported.

2. **Click "Add Expense" or "New Transaction":** Look for a button or link that says "Add Expense" or something

similar. This will open a new form for you to fill in the details.

3. **Fill in the Details:** You'll be prompted to enter:

   o **Date:** When the expense occurred.

   o **Vendor:** Who you paid (e.g., a store name, service provider, or individual).

   o **Category:** Choose a category that fits the expense, like "Groceries," "Utilities," or "Office Supplies." These categories help organize your spending later.

   o **Amount:** The total cost of the expense.

   o **Notes:** Any extra details that might help you remember the context of the expense (optional).

4. **Save Your Entry:** Once you've entered all the details, click "Save." Your expense is now recorded and will appear in your expense reports.

Tips to Keep Manual Entries Stress-Free

- **Keep Receipts Organized:** Maintain a simple filing system for your receipts, whether it's a physical folder or a digital one. This makes it easier to find the information you need when entering expenses.

- **Regular Updates:** Try to record your expenses soon after they occur. Keeping your records updated regularly will make the task less overwhelming and ensure your data is always current.

- **Review Your Entries:** Take a few moments each week to review your manual entries. This helps catch any errors early and gives you a clearer picture of your spending habits.

Tracking your expenses doesn't have to be a headache. By connecting your bank account safely, you can automate much of the process, while manual entry fills in the gaps when needed. QuickBooks Online is designed to simplify these tasks with clear instructions and a user-friendly interface, so you can keep a close eye on your spending without feeling overwhelmed.

Categorizing Your Spending (The Simple Way)

One of the secrets to managing your finances effortlessly is knowing where your money is going. Categorizing your spending helps you keep your records neat, understand your habits, and spot areas where you might save a little extra. Here's how to do it without any confusion:

1. Why Categorize?

- **Clarity:** Categorizing gives you a clear picture of your expenses. Instead of a jumbled list of numbers, you see organized groups like groceries, utilities, and healthcare. This clarity helps you see where you're spending the most and where you might adjust.

- **Ease of Management:** When your expenses are neatly organized, it's much easier to prepare for tax time, set budgets, and review your overall financial health.

2. Setting Up Categories in QuickBooks Online

- **Pre-Defined Categories:** QuickBooks Online comes with a set of pre-defined categories. These cover common expenses such as "Food," "Rent," "Utilities," "Transportation," and more. These ready-made options are designed to be straightforward and easy to understand.

- **Custom Categories:** If the pre-set options don't perfectly match your spending, you can create custom categories. For example, if you have a regular expense that doesn't fit neatly into an existing category—like "Gardening Supplies" or "Hobbies"—feel free to add a new category. This way, every expense finds its proper home.

- **Using Simple Names:** When naming your categories, choose words that make sense to you. The goal is to have labels that immediately remind you what the expense is about, without any confusing accounting jargon.

3. How to Categorize While Recording an Expense

- **During Entry:** Whether you're entering expenses automatically from your bank or manually adding them, you'll see an option to select a category. Take a moment to choose the one that best fits the expense. This might be as simple as selecting "Groceries" for your weekly shopping or "Medical" for a doctor's visit.

- **Review and Edit:** Over time, if you find that a certain expense was placed in the wrong category, don't worry—it's easy to go back and adjust. Regularly reviewing your transactions helps ensure everything is in its right place.

Tip: Try setting aside a few minutes at the end of the week to review your expenses. This regular check-in makes the task less overwhelming and keeps your financial records tidy.

Viewing Expense Reports You Can Understand

Once you've organized your expenses, it's important to see the bigger picture. QuickBooks Online transforms your raw data into simple, easy-to-read reports that help you understand how you're spending your money.

1. What Are Expense Reports?

- **Snapshot of Your Spending:** Expense reports summarize your spending over a selected period—daily, weekly, monthly, or yearly. Think of these reports as your financial progress reports that highlight where your money is going.

- **Visual and Clear:** The reports often include charts, graphs, or color-coded sections. This visual presentation makes it easier to grasp trends at a glance, even if you're not a numbers expert.

2. How to View and Interpret Your Expense Reports

- **Accessing Reports:** From your dashboard, navigate to the "Reports" section and select the expense report that interests you. QuickBooks Online offers a variety of report types; choose one that provides a clear view of your spending.

- **Understanding the Layout:** Most expense reports will list your spending by category, showing the total amount spent in each. For example, you might see "Groceries – $500," "Utilities – $150," and "Entertainment – $80." This breakdown makes it easy to see which areas are your biggest expenses.

- **Using Visual Aids:** Look for pie charts or bar graphs that break down your spending. These visual tools help you quickly understand which categories take up the largest portion of your budget. A pie chart, for example, might show that groceries make up 40% of your total expenses, while utilities cover 15%.

3. Customizing Your Expense Reports

- **Date Range Selection:** Adjust the date range to see different snapshots of your spending. Compare your expenses month-to-month, or review a full year to spot long-term trends.

- **Filtering by Category:** If you want to focus on a particular area, such as healthcare expenses, you can filter the report to show just that category. This makes it easier to analyze and understand specific parts of your spending.

- **Large Print and Clear Labels:** The reports are designed with clarity in mind. With options for larger text and straightforward labels, you can review your financial data without any hassle.

Tip: Use these reports as a conversation starter with yourself. Ask questions like, "Do I notice any surprises in my spending?" or "Is there an area where I can trim a little expense?" This reflective approach makes financial management less about numbers and more about understanding your habits.

Wrapping Up

Tracking your expenses and making sense of them is a cornerstone of effective financial management. By categorizing your spending in a simple way and reviewing expense reports that are designed for clarity, you're empowering yourself to see the whole picture of your financial health.

Take your time to set up your categories and explore the reports. With each review, you'll grow more confident in understanding your money and making informed decisions. Remember, this process is about making your life easier and more secure—one step at a time, without the stress or confusion.

You're doing a fantastic job on your journey to financial clarity. Keep up the great work, and know that every little step you take brings you closer to complete financial confidence.

CHAPTER FIVE

Organizing Your Finances

Welcome to Chapter 5! In this section, we're going to focus on bringing order to your financial world. Whether you're managing personal expenses or a small business budget, a little organization goes a long way. In this chapter, you'll learn how to use categories and tags to neatly sort your transactions and how to keep track of recurring payments without any stress. Let's dive in and make your finances work for you in the simplest way possible.

Using Categories and Tags

Imagine your finances as a well-organized filing cabinet. Each document has its place, making it easy to find what you need when you need it. In QuickBooks Online, categories and tags serve this purpose, grouping your transactions so you can quickly understand your spending habits.

Why Categories and Tags Matter

- **Easy Organization:** Categories are like folders in your filing cabinet—they group similar expenses together. For instance, all your grocery expenses might be under "Food," while your utility bills fall under "Utilities."

Tags are like sticky notes that add extra details. They let you highlight specifics that might cut across multiple categories, such as marking expenses that are related to a particular project or event.

- **Clear Financial Picture:** When your transactions are sorted with clear labels, you can instantly see where your money is going. This clarity is invaluable for planning budgets, preparing for tax time, or simply understanding your spending patterns.

- **Flexibility and Customization:** You aren't forced to stick with one set of categories. QuickBooks Online comes with pre-defined options, but you can always create custom categories and tags to fit your unique needs. Whether you're tracking hobby-related expenses or splitting household bills, there's a way to label it that makes sense to you.

How to Use Categories and Tags in QuickBooks Online

- **During Transaction Entry:** Whenever you enter an expense or income item, you'll have an option to assign a category. Simply choose the one that best fits the transaction—like "Dining Out" for a restaurant bill or "Medical" for a doctor's visit. If necessary, add a tag to provide further context (for example, "Monthly Subscription" or "Home Renovation").

- **Review and Adjust:** Over time, you might find that certain transactions need to be moved to a different category or that a new tag might help clarify things further. QuickBooks Online makes it easy to go back and edit these details. This ongoing review ensures your records always reflect your current financial picture.

Tip: Think of categories as the broad buckets that organize your money, while tags add that extra detail to help you understand the finer points of your spending. The more accurately you label your transactions, the easier it will be to analyze and manage your finances.

Keeping Track of Recurring Payments

Recurring payments are those regular expenses or incomes that happen on a set schedule—like your monthly utilities, subscriptions, or even rental income. Keeping track of these payments is crucial because they form the steady heartbeat of your financial routine.

Why Recurring Payments are Important

- **Budgeting and Planning:** Knowing exactly when your recurring bills come in and go out helps you plan your monthly budget. This foresight prevents surprises and ensures you're always prepared for regular expenses.

- **Automatic Reminders:** When you set up recurring payments in QuickBooks Online, you can benefit from automatic reminders and entries. This way, you never miss a due date, which helps protect your credit and maintains a smooth financial flow.

Setting Up Recurring Payments in QuickBooks Online

- **Find the Recurring Transactions Feature:** Look for the "Recurring Transactions" option in your QuickBooks Online menu. This feature is designed to handle those regular payments with minimal effort on your part.

- **Create a Recurring Payment Template:** Once you're in the recurring transactions section, you can create a template for each regular expense or income. You'll need to specify details like the payment amount, frequency (weekly, monthly, etc.), and the date it should recur.

- **Review and Confirm Details:** Make sure that all the information is correct. For example, check that the correct category is applied and that the payment date aligns with your schedule. Once set, QuickBooks Online will automatically record these transactions for you.

Tip: Take a few minutes once a month to review your recurring transactions. This simple step ensures that everything is up-to-date and that there are no surprises when your bills are due.

Organizing your finances doesn't have to be a complicated process. By using categories and tags, you can create a clear, intuitive filing system that helps you understand where your money is going. And by keeping track of recurring payments, you can plan your budget with confidence and avoid any last-minute rushes.

Budgeting Tools for Personal and Business Use

Creating a budget is like drawing a map for your financial journey. It shows you where your money is coming from and where it's going, helping you plan for the future without any surprises. QuickBooks Online offers a variety of budgeting tools that can be tailored to your unique needs, whether you're managing household expenses, running a small business, or juggling both.

Why Use Budgeting Tools?

- **Gain Clarity:** A budget provides a clear picture of your income versus your spending. It helps you understand your financial habits, so you can make informed decisions about where to cut back or invest a little more.

- **Plan for the Future:** Whether you're saving for a vacation, planning to pay off a loan, or simply trying to keep your bills in check, a budget acts as a roadmap. It shows you what's necessary and what can be adjusted along the way.

- **Reduce Financial Stress:** Knowing that you have a plan in place can significantly ease the worry about unexpected expenses or overspending. It's all about building confidence in your money management skills.

How to Set Up a Budget in QuickBooks Online

1. **Access the Budgeting Tool:** From your dashboard, locate the budgeting section. This might be found under "Reports" or "Planning," depending on the layout. The interface is designed to be straightforward and user-friendly.

2. **Choose Your Budget Type:**

- o **Personal Budgets:** If you're managing household finances, you can set up a budget to track monthly expenses like groceries, utilities, and entertainment.

- o **Business Budgets:** For those managing a small business, you can create separate budgets for different aspects of your operations, such as sales, marketing, or office expenses.

3. **Input Your Data:** Enter your estimated income and planned expenses. QuickBooks Online might offer suggestions based on previous transactions, which can be especially helpful if you're new to budgeting.

4. **Review and Adjust:** Once your budget is set, review the figures. The budgeting tool often displays your data in clear graphs or charts, making it easy to see if you're on track. Remember, a budget isn't set in stone—it's a flexible plan that you can adjust as your financial situation changes.

Tip: Spend a few minutes at the start of each month reviewing your budget. This small habit can help you catch any discrepancies early and keep you aligned with your financial goals.

Setting Reminders and Alerts

Even the best budget or financial plan can go awry if important dates slip your mind. That's where reminders and alerts come in. QuickBooks Online lets you set up notifications that keep you informed about key financial activities, ensuring that nothing falls through the cracks.

Why Reminders and Alerts Are Essential

- **Never Miss a Payment:** With recurring bills and scheduled transactions, a missed payment can create unnecessary stress. Reminders help you stay on top of due dates, so you can avoid late fees or disruptions in service.

- **Stay Organized:** Alerts can notify you when important financial events occur, such as when a bank transaction has been recorded or when it's time to review your budget. They're like gentle nudges that keep you moving forward.

- **Reduce Worry:** Knowing that you have a system in place to remind you of upcoming expenses or important tasks can give you peace of mind. You'll feel more secure in your financial management and less burdened by the small details.

How to Set Up Reminders and Alerts in QuickBooks Online

1. **Find the Notifications Section:** Look for a "Reminders" or "Alerts" option in your account settings or dashboard. This area is typically designed to be easy to navigate, even if you're not very tech-savvy.

2. **Choose What to Monitor:** You can set alerts for a variety of activities, such as:

   o **Bill Payments:** Receive a reminder a few days before a bill is due.

   o **Recurring Transactions:** Get notifications when a recurring payment is processed.

   o **Budget Reviews:** Set a monthly reminder to review your budget and adjust if needed.

3. **Customize Your Alerts:** Decide how you'd like to receive these notifications—via email, within the app, or both. Adjust the timing so that the reminders come at a moment that suits your schedule.

4. **Test and Tweak:** Once your alerts are set up, monitor them for a couple of weeks. If you find that you're getting too many notifications or not enough, adjust the

settings until you find the perfect balance that works for you.

Tip: Write down your key financial dates in a physical calendar or a digital one that syncs with your QuickBooks alerts. This dual approach can help reinforce your schedule and ensure you never miss an important payment or review session.

Wrapping Up

Organizing your finances with budgeting tools and timely reminders is all about creating a system that supports your financial well-being. By setting up a clear budget, you gain a roadmap to guide your spending, while reminders and alerts keep you on track every day.

Remember, the goal isn't to overwhelm you with numbers and notifications—it's to provide simple, effective tools that make managing your money easier and more enjoyable. With these strategies in place, you'll have more time to focus on what truly matters in life, confident that your finances are well-organized and under control.

You're doing a fantastic job taking these steps toward financial clarity. Each small adjustment builds a stronger foundation for your future, one that's as stress-free and empowering as possible. Keep going—you've got this!

CHAPTER SIX

Reconciling Bank Statements—Step by Step

Welcome to Chapter 6! You're doing a fantastic job navigating QuickBooks Online so far. Now it's time to talk about a simple but important task: **reconciling your bank statements**.

Don't let the word "reconcile" scare you—it's just a fancy way of saying, *"Let's make sure the numbers in QuickBooks match what's in your bank account."* Think of it like balancing your checkbook the way you might have done for years—only now, QuickBooks helps do most of the work for you.

What Is Reconciliation and Why It Matters

Reconciliation is simply comparing what's in your QuickBooks with what your bank says happened—like checking off items on a list to make sure they match.

Here's why it's a good habit to get into:

- **You catch mistakes early.** Maybe something was entered twice, or maybe you missed recording a payment.

- **You avoid surprises.** When QuickBooks matches your real-world account, you know *exactly* how much money you really have.

- **You gain peace of mind.** There's a certain comfort in knowing your books are tidy and accurate.

- **It helps at tax time.** Whether you're doing your taxes or handing them off to someone else, clean books make things easier.

Think of reconciliation as a financial check-up—and just like going to the doctor, the more regular you are about it, the better things run.

Step-by-Step: How to Reconcile

Let's take it nice and slow—step by step—with plenty of plain English.

Step 1: Get Your Bank Statement Ready

Before you start, grab your most recent **bank statement** (paper or digital). You'll need:

- The **ending balance** (how much money was in your account at the end of the month)

- The **ending date** (usually the last day of the month)

Step 2: Log Into QuickBooks Online

- Open your web browser and go to QuickBooks Online.

- Sign in with your email and password.

Step 3: Go to the Reconcile Tool

Here's how to find it:

1. Look at the **left-hand menu**.

2. Click on **"Transactions"**, then select **"Reconcile."**

3. Choose the **bank account** you want to reconcile (for example, your checking or savings).

Step 4: Enter the Statement Info

QuickBooks will ask for a few details:

- **Ending balance:** Type the amount shown on your bank statement.

- **Ending date:** Enter the final date from your statement.

Click **"Start Reconciling."**

Step 5: Match Your Transactions

Now, QuickBooks shows you a list of all the income and expenses recorded.

Here's what you do:

- **Compare each transaction** in QuickBooks to what's on your bank statement.

- If they match, click the ✔**checkmark** next to it.

- If you see something that's on your bank statement but not in QuickBooks, don't worry. You can **add it manually** by clicking "+ New" at the top and entering the transaction.

- If something's in QuickBooks but not on your bank statement, double-check to make sure it wasn't a mistake or a future-dated payment.

Take your time—there's no rush.

Step 6: Review the Difference

As you go, QuickBooks will show a small box that says **"Difference."**

Your goal is to make that number **zero**. That means everything matches perfectly.

If there's a small difference (like a bank fee or interest), you can add an **adjustment** by clicking the "Add Adjustment" link.

Step 7: Finish and Save

Once the difference is **zero** and everything looks good, click **"Finish Now."**

QuickBooks will save your work and create a **reconciliation report**—a summary of what you just did. You can print it or save it for your records.

Quick Tips to Remember

- **Reconcile monthly.** Doing it once a month keeps things simple and quick.

- **Don't panic over differences.** Even the pros run into mismatches. Just take your time.

- **Use the Help Button.** If you're stuck, click the little question mark (?) at the top right—QuickBooks will guide you.

Reconciling your bank account might sound intimidating at first, but once you do it a few times, it becomes second nature. And with QuickBooks doing most of the heavy lifting, it's easier than ever to keep your finances in good shape.

Fixing Common Mistakes (It's Easier Than You Think!)

Even the most experienced folks slip up now and then—maybe you clicked the wrong date, added a duplicate entry, or forgot to categorize something. No worries! Here's how to catch and fix those little bumps in the road.

1. A Transaction Is Missing from Reconciliation

Problem: Your bank shows a transaction, but it's not in QuickBooks.

Fix:

- Click **+ New** (top left).

- Choose the correct type (e.g., expense or deposit).

- Enter the date, amount, and other details from your bank statement.

- Save it, and then go back to reconcile.

You should now see that transaction ready to check off!

2. A Duplicate Transaction Shows Up

Problem: You see the same transaction twice in QuickBooks.

Fix:

- Go to **Transactions** > **Banking**.

- Find the duplicate.

- Click on it, then click **Delete** (you may need to click the pencil icon to edit first).

Just like that, it's gone.

3. The Wrong Amount Was Entered

Problem: You entered the right transaction but used the wrong number.

Fix:

- Find the transaction under **Transactions** > **Expenses** or **Sales**.

- Click on the entry.

- Click the **pencil icon** to edit.

- Fix the number and save.

4. The Difference Won't Go to Zero

If the difference just won't balance, try this:

- Double-check the **starting and ending balance** you entered from your bank statement.

- Make sure you **checked off every transaction** that appears on your bank statement.

- Look out for small charges like **bank fees** or **interest earned**—these often sneak in!

If you're still stuck, take a break and come back with fresh eyes—or use the **Help button (?)** in the top right corner of your screen. QuickBooks can walk you through it.

Staying on Top of Monthly Reviews

Now that you've got the hang of reconciliation, let's make it part of your monthly routine. It doesn't have to be a big event—just a calm, simple check-in with your money.

Set a Regular Review Day

Pick a day that's easy to remember. Maybe the **first Monday of each month** or the day after your bank statement arrives. Add a sticky note on the fridge or a reminder on your calendar.

Consistency is key!

What to Check Each Month

Here's a quick list you can follow:

1. **Open QuickBooks Online** and go to **Reconcile.**

2. **Compare your bank statement** to what's recorded in QuickBooks.

3. **Check for errors**—missing items, duplicates, or strange entries.

4. **Look at your income and expenses** for the month:

   ○ Are they what you expected?

   ○ Are you spending more in one category than usual?

   ○ Did a subscription charge more than it should?

5. **Run a report** (like the Profit & Loss report) to get a snapshot of your finances.

Tip: Keep a Notebook or Digital Note

It can help to jot down notes after each monthly review. Write what went well, anything unusual, and things you might want to ask your accountant or bookkeeper. A simple notebook or even a Word document will do the trick.

A Gentle Reminder: You're in Control

Remember, **this is your money**, and you're doing something truly powerful by taking charge of it. Every time you reconcile, fix a small mistake, or complete a monthly check-in, you're building financial confidence and clarity.

Mistakes don't mean you've failed. They're just stepping stones to understanding. And the more you practice, the smoother it gets.

Quick Recap

- **Fixing mistakes** is part of the process—don't worry!

- **Reconcile once a month** to keep things tidy and stress-free.

- **Use reminders** to build a simple, reliable routine.

- **Ask for help** when needed—QuickBooks is here to support you, and so am I!

Ready to move on? In the next chapter, we'll explore **staying organized with reports and summaries** that actually make sense.

CHAPTER SEVEN

Reports You'll Actually Use

Let's face it—most people don't get excited about reports. They sound complicated, full of accounting mumbo-jumbo, and sometimes just downright confusing. But here's the good news: **QuickBooks Online creates reports that are useful, clear, and—yes—easy to understand** once you know what to look for.

In this chapter, we'll explore the most helpful reports, explain what they mean in plain English, and show you how to **view, export, and print** them for your own records—or to share with a family member, accountant, or tax preparer.

Profit & Loss in Plain English

Let's start with one of the most helpful reports: the **Profit & Loss** report (sometimes called the "P&L").

So, what is it?

Think of it like a **snapshot of your money in and out**.

- **Profit** is what you made.

- **Loss** is what you spent.

71

- This report shows whether you made money or lost money over a certain period—like a month, quarter, or year.

Why it matters:

It helps you answer questions like:

- Am I bringing in more than I'm spending?

- Where is my money going?

- Are there areas I could cut back?

How to find it in QuickBooks Online:

1. From the left menu, click **Reports**.

2. Under **Favorites**, click **Profit and Loss**.

3. Choose a **date range** at the top (like "Last Month" or "This Year").

4. Click **Run Report**.

That's it! You'll now see your income at the top, your expenses in the middle, and your total profit (or loss) at the bottom.

Senior Tip: Use the **zoom tool on your browser** (Ctrl + "+" or Command + "+") to make the report easier to read.

Balance Sheet Made Simple

Next up is the **Balance Sheet**. Don't worry—this sounds more complex than it really is.

In plain terms:

The balance sheet shows what you **own** (your assets), what you **owe** (your liabilities), and your **net worth** (what's left after debts).

Think of it like a **financial health checkup**.

Here's what it tells you:

- How much cash or money you have in the bank

- If you owe anyone (like bills or loans)

- What your business or household is "worth" financially

To view it:

1. Click **Reports** from the left menu.

2. Look for **Balance Sheet** (you can type it in the search bar if needed).

3. Choose a **date**, such as the end of the month or year.

4. Click **Run Report**.

You'll see:

- Assets (your bank account, savings, etc.)

- Liabilities (credit cards, loans, etc.)

- Equity (what's left after debts)

Expense Summaries at a Glance

Want to know where your money is going each month? The **Expense Summary** or **Expenses by Vendor/Category** reports break it all down for you.

Why you'll love it:

- You'll see **how much you're spending** on things like utilities, groceries, or subscriptions.

- It shows spending **by category**, so you can spot patterns.

- Helps you **stay in control of your budget**.

How to view:

1. Go to **Reports**.

2. In the search box, type "Expenses by Vendor Summary" or "Expenses by Category."

3. Set the **date range**—try "Last 30 Days" or "This Year."

4. Click **Run Report**.

You'll now see who's getting your money and how much. Very handy!

Exporting and Printing Reports

Once you've looked at a report, you may want to **save it, print it, or email it** to someone you trust.

To print or save a report:

1. Open any report (like Profit & Loss or Balance Sheet).

2. At the top right, click the **"Export" icon** (it looks like a square with an arrow).

3. Choose:

   o **Export to PDF** – Good for printing or emailing

   o **Export to Excel** – Good if you or someone else wants to edit or sort the data

4. To **print**, just open the PDF and click the **printer icon**.

Senior Tip: If you want to save the report on your computer, choose **PDF** and then click "Save As" when prompted. Name it something easy to remember like "P&L_March2025.pdf."

Recap: What to Remember

- **Profit & Loss** = What you earned vs. what you spent

- **Balance Sheet** = What you own, owe, and your net worth

- **Expense Summary** = Where your money is going

- **Export/Print** = Save for your own records or to share with a helper

You're Doing Great!

Reports might sound like something only accountants love, but now you've seen that they can be simple, clear, and even empowering. When you can **see where your money's going**, you can make better decisions, stay on track, and feel more at peace with your finances.

CHAPTER EIGHT

Working with a Bookkeeper or Family Member

Let's be honest—sometimes managing finances can feel like juggling too many things at once. The good news is, **you don't have to do it all by yourself**.

Whether it's a bookkeeper, an accountant, or a trusted family member, **QuickBooks Online makes it easy to share your financial information with someone who can lend a hand—safely and securely.**

In this chapter, you'll learn how to give someone access to your QuickBooks account without giving away control, and how to **collaborate without confusion**.

Sharing Access Without Worry

Imagine having someone help you review your finances or enter data without needing to sit next to you. With QuickBooks Online, you can **invite a trusted person to your account**, and they can log in from their own computer.

The best part? **You stay in control**, and you can remove access anytime you want.

How to Invite Someone to Help:

1. **Log in to your QuickBooks Online** account.

2. Click the **Settings gear icon** (top right corner).

3. Select **Manage Users**.

4. Click the **"Add User"** button.

5. Choose the type of user:

   o If it's a bookkeeper or accountant, select **Accountant**.

   o If it's a family member helping you out, select **Standard User**.

6. Enter their **email address** and follow the prompts.

Senior Tip: The person you invite will receive an email with a link. They click it and set up their own login—easy and safe.

Permissions and Security Basics

You might be wondering:

"If I let someone in, can they see everything?"

Not unless you say so.

QuickBooks lets you **control what others can see and do.**

For example:

- A family member can help you **enter expenses** but not see your bank balances.

- An accountant can be given **full access** to review reports and taxes.

Permission Options Include:

- **All access** (great for a bookkeeper)

- **Limited access** (perfect for someone helping you with just a few tasks)

- **View-only** (safe for those you want to keep informed but not involved)

How to Adjust Permissions:

When you add or edit a user, QuickBooks will ask:

- Do you want this person to see **everything** or **specific areas only**?

- Do you want them to **make changes** or just **view** things?

Security Tip: Only share access with people you fully trust. Never give your own password. Always use the user invite feature—this keeps your information protected.

Collaborating with Someone You Trust

Whether it's your daughter, grandson, friend, or a professional bookkeeper, working together doesn't have to be stressful.

QuickBooks Online is built for teamwork. You can each log in from your own devices, and the changes update instantly—no need to email spreadsheets back and forth or worry about things getting lost.

Tips for a Smooth Collaboration:

- **Set a regular check-in** (monthly or quarterly) to go over your finances.

- **Use Notes or Memos** inside QuickBooks to leave messages for each other.

- **Review Reports together**, such as Profit & Loss or Expense Summaries.

- **Don't be afraid to ask questions**—it's your money and your peace of mind.

You can even give temporary access to someone and remove them later. This is great if someone is just helping you during tax season or for a short time.

Recap: You're Still in Control

Here's what you now know:

- You can **share access** to your QuickBooks with someone you trust—without giving them full control.

- You control **what they see and what they can do**.

- Working with a helper, whether a professional or a loved one, can make managing finances easier, less stressful, and even enjoyable.

You're Doing a Great Job!

You've made it to Chapter 8, and you're becoming more confident with every step. Learning something new—especially technology—takes courage, and you're doing it with grace.

Whether you're taking care of your own finances or supporting a small business or household, **you've earned the right to ask for help when you need it**. And now, you know exactly how to do it, safely and simply.

CHAPTER NINE

Troubleshooting and Common Mistakes

Let's face it—we all make mistakes. Whether it's clicking the wrong button, forgetting a password, or getting a bit turned around on the screen, it happens to the best of us (yes, even the pros!).

In this chapter, we'll walk through the most common issues seniors and beginners face when using QuickBooks Online—and more importantly, how to fix them **without frustration**.

What to Do If You Get Lost

You're navigating QuickBooks and suddenly... everything looks unfamiliar. Don't worry! Getting lost in a new program is totally normal. The good news is: **there's always a way back to where you need to be.**

Here's how to quickly reset and find your way:

1. **Click the Dashboard/Home Icon:** In the left-hand menu, you'll see the word **"Dashboard"** or **"Home"**. Click that, and you'll be taken back to the main screen.

2. **Use the Help Button:** In the top right corner, there's a **little question mark (?)** icon. This is your lifeline when you're unsure of what to do next.

3. **Close Tabs Inside QuickBooks:** If you see several tabs open within the program (like multiple invoices or reports), you can close them one by one to clear the screen.

Senior Tip: If all else fails, close your internet browser and reopen QuickBooks. Nothing will be lost—you can pick up right where you left off.

Fixing Duplicates and Errors

Sometimes QuickBooks records something twice. Or maybe you typed in the wrong amount by mistake. These little hiccups are common—and easy to correct.

To fix a duplicate transaction:

1. Go to the **Transactions** tab.

2. Look for two entries that look exactly the same.

3. Click one and choose **"Exclude"** or **"Delete"** (depending on what the error is).

4. Always double-check before deleting—if you're not sure, ask someone you trust or use the Help button.

To edit a mistake:

1. Click on the incorrect item (like an expense or invoice).

2. Click the **"Edit"** button.

3. Change the numbers or details.

4. Click **"Save and Close."**

Helpful Tip: QuickBooks always keeps a record of what you've done. So if you make a mistake, you can usually reverse it.

Contacting QuickBooks Support

If something just doesn't seem right and you need a friendly expert, QuickBooks has **real people who can help you**.

Here's how to reach them:

1. Click the **Help (?) icon** in the top-right corner of the screen.

2. Type your question or click **"Contact Us."**

3. You can choose to:

   o Chat with an agent

o   Schedule a callback (they'll call YOU)

o   Browse helpful articles and videos

Senior Support Tip: If you're more comfortable talking to a real person, choose the callback option. You don't have to wait on hold—they'll call you when it's your turn.

Resetting Your Password and Settings

Forgetting your password isn't the end of the world—it happens to all of us. Fortunately, QuickBooks makes resetting it **painless**.

If you forget your password:

1.   On the sign-in screen, click **"Forgot Password?"**

2.   Enter your email address.

3.   Check your email for a reset link and follow the simple steps.

Tip: If you don't see the email, check your "Spam" or "Junk" folder just in case.

To reset your settings:

Maybe you accidentally changed something and want to go back to the way things were.

1.   Click the **Settings gear icon** in the upper-right corner.

2. Choose **"Account and Settings."**

3. Browse each tab (like "Company" or "Advanced") to change things back.

4. Click **"Save"** after each change.

Don't be afraid to explore. You can't "break" QuickBooks—just take it one step at a time.

You're Doing Better Than You Think!

Every click, every question, and every small fix you make is a step forward. Learning something new isn't always easy, but **you've come this far—and that's worth celebrating**.

Remember:

- You're not alone.

- Mistakes can be fixed.

- Help is always available.

- You've got this!

Quick Recap:

- Use the **Dashboard** or **Help** button if you get lost.

- Duplicates and errors are **easy to correct**—just review carefully.

- You can **contact support** any time you feel stuck.

- Resetting your **password or settings** is safe and simple.

CHAPTER TEN

Keeping Your Information Safe

You've worked hard to get your finances in order—and now it's time to make sure everything stays safe. Just like you lock your front door before bed, you should also lock down your digital information.

Don't worry—you don't have to be a tech wizard to keep things secure. In this chapter, we'll walk you through **simple steps** to protect your QuickBooks account and financial details with confidence.

Safe Password Practices

Let's start with the key to your digital front door: your password. A good password is your first and strongest layer of protection.

Here's how to create a safe password **you can actually remember**:

- Use a mix of **uppercase and lowercase letters**, **numbers**, and **symbols**.

    Example: GrannyBakes#2025

- Avoid using personal details like your birthday or "12345."

- Use a phrase that means something to you. Example: ILoveTulips@Spring2024

Senior Tip: Write your password down and store it in a safe place, like a locked drawer. Or use a simple password notebook kept near your computer—just don't leave it lying around.

Also:

- **Never share your password** with someone you don't fully trust.

- Change your password **every few months**, just to be safe.

Recognizing Phishing and Scams

Scammers are sneaky. They might send you fake emails that *look* like they're from QuickBooks, your bank, or another trusted source. These are called **phishing emails**, and they're meant to trick you into giving away personal info.

Here's how to spot a scam:

- The email says something urgent, like **"Your account is in danger!"**

- It asks you to click a strange link or **enter your password.**

- The email **spelling or grammar** seems off or unprofessional.

- The sender's email address looks suspicious or has extra characters.

If you're unsure:

- **Do not click the link.**

- Open a new browser tab and **type www.quickbooks.intuit.com** yourself.

- Or call a family member or QuickBooks support to double-check.

Senior Safety Reminder: QuickBooks will never ask for your password in an email. If something feels "off," it probably is.

Backing Up Your Data

One of the best things about QuickBooks Online is that **your data is backed up automatically** in the cloud. That means if your computer crashes or you spill coffee on your keyboard, your finances are safe.

Still, it's a smart idea to back up your reports manually now and then, just for peace of mind.

How to back up your reports:

1. Go to **Reports** from the left menu.

2. Choose your report (like Profit & Loss or Expenses).

3. Click **"Export"** at the top right.

4. Select **Excel** or **PDF**.

5. Save it to a USB drive or your computer.

Bonus Tip: Keep backups on a USB flash drive labeled "QuickBooks Reports" and store it somewhere safe, like a desk drawer or safe box.

Two-Factor Authentication for Seniors

Two-factor authentication (or 2FA) sounds fancy, but it's really just an extra layer of protection. Think of it like a second lock on your front door.

Here's how it works:

1. You log in with your email and password.

2. QuickBooks sends a special code to your phone or email.

3. You type in that code to get access.

It's quick, easy, and adds **strong protection** against hackers.

To turn it on:

1. Click the **Gear icon (⚙)** > Choose **Account and Settings**.

2. Select **Security**.

3. Click **Two-Step Verification** and follow the prompts.

4. You'll enter your phone number and get a test code.

Senior Tip: If you don't have a smartphone, choose the **email** option instead of text messages.

Quick Recap

- **Strong passwords** keep your account safe. Use phrases you'll remember!

- Watch out for **phishing emails**—if it feels odd, don't click.

- **Back up your reports** to your computer or a USB drive.

- **Enable Two-Factor Authentication** for double security.

Keeping your finances safe doesn't mean you have to be a tech expert. It just takes a few smart habits, and you've already learned them in this chapter!

By setting up your security and staying alert, you're making sure that **your financial information stays in your hands—and only yours.**

BONUS 1

Quick Start Checklist

If you're the type who likes to have a step-by-step list **right in front of you**, this bonus is just for you. This **Quick Start Checklist** takes the mystery out of setting up QuickBooks Online and gets you started without frustration.

Tip: Print this page out and keep it next to your computer. You can even check off each box as you go!

Step-by-Step Setup Guide

1. Sign In or Create Your QuickBooks Account

☐ Go to www.quickbooks.intuit.com

☐ Click **Sign In** if you already have an account

☐ Or click **Start Free Trial** to create a new account

☐ Enter your name, email, and create a strong password

2. Answer a Few Simple Questions

☐ QuickBooks will ask about your business or personal use

☐Choose what best fits your needs (you can update later)

☐ Give your account a name—like "Grandma's Finances" or "Smith Household"

☐Choose your currency (usually U.S. dollars)

3. Take a Quick Tour of the Dashboard

☐Look for the **left-hand menu** (this is your command center!)

☐Click around slowly—Home, Sales, Expenses, Banking

☐Don't worry—nothing breaks if you just explore!

4. Connect Your Bank Account (Optional But Helpful)

☐Go to **Banking**

☐Click **Connect Account**

☐Choose your bank and sign in securely

☐ QuickBooks will pull in your recent transactions for easy tracking

5. Enter a Test Transaction

☐ Go to + **New** (top-left of the dashboard)

☐ Click **Invoice** or **Expense**

☐ Fill in basic info (you can make this one up to practice!)

☐ Save and close—just to get the feel for it

6. Customize Your Settings for Ease

☐ Click the **Gear Icon (☐)** in the top right

☐ Choose **Account and Settings**

☐ Adjust font size in your browser or use Zoom to make text bigger

☐ Set your time zone, business info, and notification preferences

7. Set Up Categories for Organizing

☐ Go to **Settings > Chart of Accounts**

☐ Review or create categories like "Utilities," "Medical," or "Donations"

☐These help you track where your money is going

8. Bookmark QuickBooks in Your Browser

☐Open QuickBooks Online in your internet browser

☐ Click the **star icon** (top right of most browsers) to save as a favorite

☐Name it something easy like "My QuickBooks"

Extra Tip: Print Your Reports Easily

☐Go to **Reports** on the left-hand side

☐Choose one (Profit & Loss, Expenses, etc.)

☐Click **Export > PDF**

☐Print and save in a binder labeled "Finances"

This checklist is designed to help you **start with confidence**. Don't worry if it takes a few tries to get used to everything— QuickBooks Online was made to make life *easier*, not harder.

If something feels confusing, take a deep breath, refer back to this list, or ask a family member or bookkeeper to guide you through it. **You've got this.**

BONUS 2

Common Terms Made Simple

Let's face it—**accounting can sound like a foreign language.** Words like "accounts payable" and "reconciliation" might make your head spin. But don't worry! This bonus glossary breaks down **common QuickBooks and accounting terms** into plain English.

It's written just for **you**—the senior or non-tech-savvy user who wants to understand things **without a dictionary** or a Google search.

A–Z of Accounting Terms in Plain English

A

Account – A place to keep track of money coming in or going out.

Example: Think of it like labeled envelopes—one for "Groceries," one for "Utilities," etc.

Assets – Things you own that have value, like a house, car, or money in the bank.

Example: Your savings account and your old but still-working laptop are assets.

B

Balance Sheet – A snapshot of what you own (assets), what you owe (debts), and what's left over.

Example: It's like taking inventory of your home—what's in, what's out, and what's yours.

Bank Feed – A live connection between QuickBooks and your bank.

Example: It's like a mailbox that gets new transaction letters every day.

C

Categories – Labels you give to transactions, like "Rent," "Gas," or "Donations."

Example: Just like sorting mail into bills, birthday cards, and coupons.

Credit – Money that comes **into** your account or reduces what you owe.

Example: A refund from the store shows up as a credit.

D

Debits – Money that goes **out** of your account.
Example: When you pay your phone bill, it's a debit.

Double-entry bookkeeping – A system where each transaction affects at least two accounts.

Example: If you spend $50 at the store, one account (cash) goes down and another (groceries) goes up.

E

Expenses – Money you spend.

Example: Your electric bill, your prescription medicine, even your newspaper subscription.

Equity – What you truly own, after subtracting debts from your assets.

Example: If your house is worth $200,000 and you owe $50,000 on it, your equity is $150,000.

I

Invoice – A bill you send someone when they owe you money.

Example: Like when your neighbor pays you to sew curtains— you can send an invoice to get paid.

Income – Money you receive.

Example: Pensions, social security, rental income—all are income.

L

Liabilities – What you owe to others.

Example: A credit card balance or a car loan.

Ledger – A record book of all your financial activity.

Example: It's like a journal where every dollar you spend or earn gets a page.

P

Profit & Loss Report (P&L) – Shows what you earned and what you spent over time.

Example: Like your checkbook register, it tells you if you're ahead or behind financially.

R

Reconciliation – Matching your QuickBooks transactions with your bank statement.

Example: Like balancing your checkbook to make sure everything adds up.

Recurring Transaction – Payments or income that happen regularly.

Example: Your Netflix bill or your monthly retirement income.

T

Transaction – Any movement of money in or out.

Example: Buying a coffee = one transaction. Paying the electric bill = another transaction.

Tags – Extra labels to organize your transactions even more.

Example: You might tag something as "Medical" or "Vacation."

V

Vendor – A person or business you pay for goods or services.

Example: The gardener, the grocery store, or your plumber—all are vendors.

Bonus Term

Two-Factor Authentication – An extra layer of security when signing in.

Example: You enter your password, and then QuickBooks sends a text to your phone to double-check it's you.

Don't worry about memorizing everything. Just keep this glossary handy. Any time a term makes you go "Huh?", come back here. These simple definitions and real-life examples will keep you grounded and feeling confident.

You're not alone. Everyone gets confused by "finance talk" at first. But with this cheat sheet, **you've got the upper hand.**

CONCLUSION

First off—**congratulations!** If you've made it to the end of this book, then you've done something truly impressive. You've stepped up, taken on something new, and proven that **age is no barrier to learning.** Whether you're 60, 70, 80, or older—you're now more in control of your finances than ever before.

QuickBooks Online might have looked a little intimidating at first, but now? **You've tamed the beast.** You've learned how to track income, record expenses, view reports, and maybe even work with a family member or bookkeeper with confidence. You've gotten the tools, the know-how, and most importantly—the **courage** to manage your money on your terms.

Where to Go From Here

This guide was just your starting point. Here's what you can do next:

- **Keep practicing.** The more often you log in and check things, the more comfortable it'll become.

- **Explore more features.** QuickBooks Online has extra tools like mileage tracking, mobile apps, and tax prep features. Dip your toes in when you're ready.

- **Lean on your support system.** Whether it's a helpful adult child, a grandchild, a trusted bookkeeper, or QuickBooks customer support—**you are never alone.**

And don't forget about your **BONUSES!** Keep that printable checklist, glossary, and any notes you've made nearby. They're your friendly tools anytime you need a refresher.

Staying Confident with Your Finances

Remember, being in charge of your finances doesn't mean you have to do everything perfectly. It means you know what's going on and feel good about your choices. That peace of mind? It's priceless.

Every time you categorize an expense, send an invoice, or simply log in and take a look at your dashboard—you're building confidence. You're staying sharp. And you're proving to yourself and the world that **you've still got it.**

A Final Word from Me to You

Thank you for allowing me to guide you on this journey. Writing this book for you wasn't just about explaining software—it was about **empowering people** who deserve to feel in control of their lives and money.

You're not just learning QuickBooks.

You're showing up.

You're taking charge.

And you're doing it with grace, curiosity, and courage.

So go ahead—**open up QuickBooks Online, log in, and give it a go.** Even if it's just five minutes today. You've got everything you need.

And remember:

If you ever get stuck… just go back to the chapters, use the Help button, or ask someone you trust. You're never too old to learn—and you're never alone on the journey.

www.ingramcontent.com/pod-product-compliance
Lightning Source LLC
LaVergne TN
LVHW051709050326
832903LV00032B/4090